PARANORMAL

NEW TESTAMENT

CELESTIAL and Beautiful APOCALYPSE

LINDA J SMITH PIPPIN

iUniverse, Inc.
Bloomington

PARANORMAL NEW TESTAMENT
CELESTIAL And Beautiful APOCALYPSE

iUniverse books may be ordered through booksellers or by contacting:

iUniverse
1663 Liberty Drive
Bloomington, IN 47403
www.iuniverse.com
1-800-Authors (1-800-288-4677)

Because of the dynamic nature of the Internet, any web addresses or links contained in this book may have changed since publication and may no longer be valid. The views expressed in this work are solely those of the author and do not necessarily reflect the views of the publisher, and the publisher hereby disclaims any responsibility for them.

Any people depicted in stock imagery provided by Thinkstock are models, and such images are being used for illustrative purposes only.

Certain stock imagery © Thinkstock.

ISBN: 978-1-4759-7154-5 (sc)
ISBN: 978-1-4759-7155-2 (e)

Printed in the United States of America

iUniverse rev. date: 1/17/2013

Biography

Born and grew up in south west Missouri.

Married fifty five years to husband Clell.

An " A " personality   mother of five, always on a project.

From Music to Painting to Poetry and Scripture research.

Nothing ever as important as God and Family.

My degree comes from life experiences,

and guidance of the Holy Spirit.

Study was never enough rightly dividing the word

As scripture says disecting the word

(About my book) " A Paranormal Bible Apocalypse"

Is filled with word apocalypses, that shed light on truth of
poor bible translation , that have also led to divisions or denominating.
of Gods people. it does discredit religion and places it in a
adversary   position to " Christian Faith" and in my opinion
will disguise   the Mark or Stigma so dreaded in John's Apocalypse.

It sets clearly where God is and our place with God.

It is best read after a Revelation study where questions arise about Symbols, such as   Waters , Trump's , Spirits ,

And Paranormal activity as everything
that is Spiritual,

ACKNOWLEDGMENTS

After years of study and at   times
mind   boggling   experiences.
My   Sweet husband Clell   " Who I love
"

has tolerated , my unusual personality
and supported one project after another .
He has been a   Blessing.

DEDICATION

To my Daughter   Sonya Kay Lewis
who grew up,   with   my   sometimes
radical ways ,
and   remained my loving little girl.
Love always.

John's Revelation He Received

On the island of Patmos has left me impressed with the way John described the vision using symbols of his

day. Reference to things he understood, to define what he saw of future events.

The understanding that John had been given was far beyond understanding of his day.

He was told to write , and his vision told that the readers will be blessed. By this we know that it was

meant to be understood.   For that time it was Paranormal   nothing he had saw before.

Apocalypse strikes fear in many , when in fact it was a beautiful time for John.

He was on this island waiting for word from God,

expecting to hear from God, and everything he heard , was for God's people . a real Revelation or

unveiling of things to come, past, present and future.

But when I see the word Apocalypse on a book cover or movie

title I know immediately. It's going to be a horror of some sort. This was not God's plan. This text of my

revelations , my apocalypses ,will be beautiful and warm instead of fearful and scary.

John was one of God's own . Many are preparing for the bad days of the Apocalypse, not sure how this

came about. There are some events of end times in the latter part of John's Revelation when the Vials are

poured out and none of God's children are there. They have already been rescued. Apocalypse as translated into Revelation was a good translation what I call a light bulb moment and uncovering or

unveiling, revealing, and a few of these I have had ,and they have always been a blessing ,

you learn something new. Or you understand something old. If the New Testament , would have been

written today it would seem not quite as paranormal.

God is not the author of confusion clearly the tiny book was not for those of John's day it would be kept

until the ending of the vision had been completed, there was a warning added at the end of this book not to

add or take away, and yet the warning itself was added by translators. Symbols were used. Then, as well

symbols now are in fact the best representation , John could give of the of what he saw. Can we imagine what

someone from 2000 years ago would feel, waking up in today's world with no knowledge of the modern world what we might call a space ship a bomb a Television or Computer we clearly understand today

better than they would have then. And at the same time some of the words use those days, are hard to

understand now.

If the translation English had been consistent it would have helped. However words from

Latin Hebrew, Greek are used when translated into English. The Hebrew word Messiah the Greek word

Christ both meant anointed, which word was used in the text, dependent on the translator. Many words

translated that way .way, such as church, which was the called out collectively

Angels & Messengers of God

.Another word in Latin or Greek was Angel translated into English is messenger. These Angels have

become very mystical, having wings here on earth. The Bible does not say that Angels have wings.

A elderly minister at one time told m the Angel he saw I had wings. My reply was, sir, I did not say your

Angels didn't have wings. I said the Bible does not say they have wings. Michel Angelo put wings on

Angels in the Sistine Chapel. Since that time, everyone has assumed Angels had wings. As a child I used to wonder if those Angels didn't get tired, flying and flapping their wings . Seem to me they would get

tired,   but no not in heaven no one gets tired. Why would Angels have to work so hard. Then, seeing

references to angels throughout the Bible,

I began to realize the people had considered Paul a Angel of God.

"And he was"   he was a messenger. And as I go along. You will see messengers play

a big part in John's Apocalypse , Revelation, or light-bulb moment.

There would've been no reason for John to have wrote his letter in English.

Who would have read   it .   I do not think there were English-speaking people there

MY PURPOSE

My purpose here on earth I think,
Not just to be born and die.
But to cause the tide of life to Nudge
from   side to side. And if I am successfull
when This life I'd done,
I'll have touched the lives of many ' and
for the good changed even one.

L.J.P.

Paul had earlier gave instruction, that we would have messengers, false messengers, in Paul's

letters   he gave a really clear warning, that we should not accept any letters said to be from Paul

that was not sealed with a kiss and salute.

"Apocalypse"--- First Timothy did not salute or kiss.

Many words used in Timothy, Paul never used in any other writing

years ago this was revealed to me. And in fear of contradicting King

James Bible . I kept silent about this Apocalypse till one day I visited the Bible bookstore came

There was confirmation of what I had revealed to me. being truth.

It had been written many years ago, and the same determination were by scholars ,

And a Scholar I was not .

Now my faith had really grown. God with me his spirit, was teaching me, and I was loving it

False Messengers

God knew Strong's Exhaustive Concordance, The King James Bible with the interlinear book of ancient Greeks Scriptures. Would one day be available. His Holy Spirit would be my teacher.

"Apocalypse- "---- Many ministers, claim to have God's Holy Spirit, most of them were as hungry for the truth is I am

SILENT   WEMON

"Apocalypse - "   ---
    First Timothy, of course, was the one who recorded the women should be silent
  churches. This did not make good sense to me. When over in Galatians, Paul says there is no
  difference in male or female, Greek or Jew.

    At the early age of 10 years old, I attended a Nazarene church for a year without missing a
  Sunday for this I was awarded a Bible. A lady handed it to me before the congregation asked me

what I wanted to be when I grew up ? In my mind the best thing I could have said was what I said

" I'd like to be a singer and a preacher"

The lady quickly respond to me by saying, "oh no, women cannot hold that office".

Now, I read ,   and I knew in myself that

"God was the father of the fatherless," and my father had died in a car wreck earlier.

I understood then that God was my father. Needless to say, my Father

and I had a long talk.   I was always aware of his love.

Many years went by A lot of trials , rocky roads . I began to know that I wasn't alone.

It is a personal search or relationship that an individual can have with God.

That includes no one but them self."

The called out of God," are those that have been called by his Holy Spirit. They

have been anointed "God's true Seal. " CHILDREN of GOD"

"

SAINTS OF GOD

Apocalypse, Holy- Saint translated from the same word

Apocalypse, same with spirit and ghost translated from the same word .These were all my Apocalypses - a Revelation, a understanding a unveiling the truth.

Many years ago I ask a elderly lady. What would I need to do to become a Saint?

She said to me " Dear you   already are a Saint"

.

Holy and Saint translated from the same word. And Gods Word says you are Holy in fact every thing that is

of God is Holy. If you think that did not empower me you should have saw how deep I began to dig for the
truth.

JOHN'S VISION

Listen to what the spirit is saying in the Church (Congregation)

John said he saw "the voice that spoke with him.

He also saw seven congregations or assemblies " OK"

Church in Asia now day Turkey.

IN THEIR MIDST APPEARED AS THE SON OF MAN. This I believe to be a flesh and blood man.

I believe he was the messenger of the people there..

And his message was for the messenger. The Angel.

The voice says to the messenger listen !
Hear what the Spirit _ Ghost is saying in
the congregation "
   CHURCH"   They were being told to
listen to the body of Christ,
   the anointed ones.   The messengers
or
   pastors   seem to act as though they are
God
   And   are   not   hearing   the   spirit
speak.
   We must know by now Jesus is the head
, we are the body.
   John fell as though he was dead .Passed
out I guess. John then is told not to be
   afraid , "I am the first and the last I am
alive forever.   I have the key to the
   place   of departed souls.   Now write
about   the past ,
   present   and   future.
   John   had   the   testimony   of Jesus
Anointing him self. But not till then had he
realized he was a part of the
   body.   Could   he   have   written   a
Paranormal   truth that could have been
   understood.   " No" .   No more than a
translation today of the Celestial body
   Jesus returned   with.

Temple

God is   self invested   into every anointed being , when they are congregated in agreement.

Their power is limitless.

Not on another planet, Not on a   cloud " IMBODIED IN HIS CHILDREN."

Notice the Voice is   clothed   of many waters. " Many People."

in John's Revelation

" Apocalypse "

Jesus said   " I am in the Father,   He is in me."

God tells us we are   the   Temple . The habitation of God.

EYES EARS AND HANDS

We know Jesus is Lord of Lords. King of kings. The head of the body .

"Where is God??" Now you know the Body is the temple. Of WHAT?

" GOD"

"This should make every Christian jump with joy."!

Would it be heresy to say we are all a tiny bit of God.?

Would it be wrong to say GOD lives in us .?

GOD SAID .

"I AM THAT I AM."EGO= I - ME -SELF

HAYA= BE -AM -IS- EXIST.

I translate ""I EXIST I SELF EXIST""!"

KING JAMES SAYS " I AM ,THAT I AM "!

Now realizing where God is. Not in another Galaxy. we should be aware that we are
the eyes and ears of God.
The prayers of saints stored up ,in the vials are our own
    prayers .
We are a Holy Priesthood , First Peter chapter 2, tells us this again a priest-hood of Saints Holy. or Holy Holly's.

No one should let any adversary to this truth , weaken their faith.
The Body of Christ is here. We are a Priesthood in this & a Celestial World.

As for some things John saw , he would have had to lived on Earth today to understand.
Horses were the main source of transporting and travel. When something was

Being carried. On a unknown vehicle.
He did not call them UFO's they were
Horses..

Most do not understand John's incredible
Apocalypse. Because it is so hard to put
our

self in John's shoes. I believe we are
embarking on the days of John's vision.

With   Cars, Planes. And   Rockets
Televisions,   Computers, Space Ships
Helicopters.

Microwaves so much   technology that
has came in just 200 years out of 2000.that
if saw

2000 years ago would have been
considered Paranormal.

Most any thing could carry biological
germs, poison gas , we should remember

Typhoid Mary even people. I am told
some smugglers of humans from south
of the

border are called Mules. I am also told
Bad means good these days to the

younger generation.

Why do we have so much trouble
communicating? " It   is in the language."

THE MARK OF THE BEAST

As we get to the Beasts we find the same barrier . One   Beast translation comes from

Therion.   meaning a out of control destroyer or Poison, it could be fiscal, or it could be a Society   , or belief , this is in Revelations chapter thirteen.

where King James translated the Mark of the Beast as 666..

as I translate. " Here wisdom exists, those having intellect , compute the calculation for mankind, and the sum of him."

(and gives three Greek Letters)

" CHI XI STIGMA   no way can I find 666 here . Hex is Greek   for   Six do not be deceived

Besides that Mark 13 :22. says even the very elect would be deceived,

" If it were possible". now if everyone is watching for 666 , who might be deceived?

Religious   people. might   if it was attached to religion.

I have always wandered why Christians are so concerned with the Mark of the Beast.

If they are sealed by God with his seal, " The Holy Spirit " We will be rejects by the

Mark of the (Therion)   Beast. He has no authority over what belongs to God.

That should make us jump for joy .

This comforter Jesus made available to us.

by reconciling us to God eternally. And Cannot   be changed, erased, voided,

For sure we need   faith,   " Without it we cannot please God "

Another Paranormal Event

Revelations chapter four and five tells of four Beasts.

(ZOON)   They are living Creatures. Full of eyes.

" Full Vision" Constantly moving not stopping day or night. I t hink you guessed it ,

Monitors, Televisions. " Full vision of things" or full of eyes. John was seeing

Past, Present , and future. Notice how John is told to come see, he had to move,

to go from one beast to the other . they were stationary.

(Ophthalmos) translated Many Eyes meant Full of Vision. Can we imagine

people walking around in a little box? Driving cars that would have been very

Paranormal then.

Symbols

We need to remember candle sticks are a symbol of a Congregation Assemblies.

There is a book of life Sealed that only Jesus can open. secure, like Locks.

Trumpets are a call to attention, These will be heard world wide .

As a Special News Report . In John's time there were town criers .

The Trump was from " Royalty " or those in charge.

A message for everyone.

With each of the seven trumps , There is world wide attention .

Every one will see.

years ago I wandered how can people on one side

of the world, see at the same time , they are seen on the opposite side of the world."

Now we know ". Television, telephones, computers, With this technology. It can be

seen world wide

FANTASIZE

LIVING IN A BUBBLE GLASS
SURROUNDING ALL.
THE ONLY WAY I CAN ESCAPE WILL
CAUSE MY WORLD TO FALL
SO I WALK ON THE CEILING,
I WALK ON THE WALL.
I FANTASIZE AND REALIZE
MY WORLDS NOT HERE AT ALL.

GODS   OR   GOD'S

Having a understanding of Jesus being Anointed , The Christ, The Messiah . A fine point
of learning how, Jesus related to God, and how we relate to
(Christ) anointing

I am sure this page will cause some to cringe. and scream " Heresy"
This is the secret , that   keep the world wrapped up in Religious Superstitions.
for over a thousand years. I always think of the Time Mary (Meriam) told Jesus they were
needing more wine for the wedding. It seemed Jesus did not think he was ready yet for a miracle, like that

that   task. but his mother did . Mary understood Jesus had Gods Spirit with out

limitations. Jesus was Anointed with Gods Spirit in Full Measure.

Jesus sent this same anointing to us by measure. We all have a Measure of Gods Spirit

Living in us . According to our measure of Faith we are "GODS "

no apostrophe.

 "What"

Collectively when we are all in unity, with God, inhabiting us, we become

Particles   of   the body of   (Christ) Anointing. Of witch Jesus is the head.

Lord of Lords ,   King of Kings. Until this is taken seriously by believers, we will not

experience the full Power of God.   Or even come to know him.

We been told God is a Spirit or Ghost, We been told he is a Spirit of Truth and Love.

and   holds   all   the knowledge of the Universe.

All the Cyber, Gurus, Eienstines,

Would have to   understand , any knowledge they had or have ,comes from the Spirit   Gods Spirit.   Eienstine was uneducated in many areas , not intelligent at all,

We have not the capability to acquire knowledge of any subject, not taught. There for it

stands to reason it has been acquired by a higher power, the Spirit " GOD"

John   chapter 10. says " IS IT NOT WRITTEN IN YOUR LAW "?

" I said you were GODS"

If he called them GODS to whom the word came, Scripture can't be broken.

Who God has sanctified and sent into this world . You blasphemed, because I said

"I am the Son of God"

If we cannot accept we are Children of God.

We are still in the mind set of John's day. Psalms 82:6   " Have said you are GODS"

again   no apostrophe.   "Not belonging to God but being God" Not supreme but a part of"

We are appointed once to die. Then the Resurrection. in the blink of a Eye we are Metamorphosed into a new creature.

the same kind of body Jesus has walks through walls , eats ,drinks

WHERE IS GODS KINGDOM?

Jesus told the disciples before his death he would not drink again

until he drinks it new in his fathers kingdom.

Then in Acts chapter 10, he did drink with

them. Confirming They were in the Kingdom of God..

As the Lord's Prayer said. Thy Kingdoms come thy will be done.

this new body, Walking through walls , would have been

a sight to see ,Thomas thrusting his hand into Jesus side.

The Greek word for Thrusting meant to Violently throw ,

Thomas hand Went right through Jesus side.

Thomas said   "My Lord My God " To Thomas this was very paranormal.

I expect Thomas   took a big breath. "My Lord My God" I would   have.!

Gods Kingdom   had   come   and Gods name had been declared,

"HAGIAZO "   Hallowed is your name. Holiest of Holly's

The Purifier, Consecrates.

This Celestial body   Jesus has is the one we are waiting for

Gods name, makes what John is hearing in Heaven .

Holy ,Holy , Holy understood. with more clarity.

WHAT SHOULD WE CALL GOD?

Mankind has many names for God . First
recorded,   Jehovah was used
        meaning" Self Existent"

Daniel called God Allah this was do to
his language. Now Arabic.

Many names for one God as someone
said,

" A Rose by any other name would still
smell like a Rose."

Supreme God not all who Worship God
have   accepted a redeemer.

Jesus said   "   There was another Fold."
He did not say who , or where,

So   I tread softly when correcting
another name for God.

FAITH WITH OUT WORKS

The adversary to truth is constantly accusing, using Superstition, Religion,
Old dogma, to cast doubt on truth. And placing a burden of Servitude on who they can
and accusations of heresy, That slowed the progress of Gods power, in the people.
A good example of this is in translation of James 2:26   " Faith with out works
is dead"   Works are important but has nothing to do with Faith.
Faith with out works should have translated (ergon -works) as using or
implementing . " Faith without use or implementing is dead.
Organized Religion cannot afford to allow faith to out weigh Works.

Yet Faith is the only way we can please God. With out it we go no where in Gods word.

" Throw the Ball in the air , this is action or works.   Knowing it will come down is Faith. How do we get that Faith? Experience, Truth, Fact, it becomes Science logic.

If you use your faith it will grow and we all have as much as a grain of mustard seed..

Many have faith in their Car Starting, that attend Church every time the doors open,

More   than they do in Gods   Word. Confidence .

MAKE SOME ONE WEALTHY
BY GIVING TO GOD

I think of Paul's statement to the Corinthians there should be no collections while he was
there.   He instructs them to take up any collections for the Saints before he arrives.
1st Cor.16"1 I often think, the messenger should feel so blessed to speak , That he
would have faith his needs would be met, with out begging " More Faith Required"
Every thing works out for the good to those who love the Lord , and are called according
to his purpose.   It is important to know what your purpose is.

Giving is between you and God, purpose in your Spirit ahead of time where and how
much you give and remember two things give in secret and be rewarded openly

Tithes is a Law of the old Testament. Remember Keep one law you are required to keep the entire Law. " That is not for me"!

U.F.O ? CELESTIAL? HEAVENLY?

Very Paranormal

" We " Those anointed with Gods Spirit, are in fact aliens in This world.

"We" anointed with A Celestial Spirit. Indwelling our flesh bodies

Our Celestial Fathers Spirit makes us , half God's and half Mankind .

And a continuous struggle between the two for dominion are on going.

There are several instances the scriptures of New Testament that give   this

understanding . Mathew 1: 22, 25 Mary must have been artificially inseminated

In order for her to remain a Virgin. A
Sleep, Joseph dreams of messenger,
Who tells Joseph the baby to be born ,
would be called ,
Emanuel meaning GOD WITH US

Then the Wise Men Astrologers and
Scientist , followed a star these were not
Kings they
Were smart men., few smart men would
travel in those days, across a Continent to
see a
Baby, who they heard was to be King of
the Jews .   Herod   the King had no
knowledge of the Child, before the Men
arrived.

Luke 2 ; 8 -15 The Shepherds in that
country, also had a encounter with
messenger 's
that same night. The witnessed a very
bright light , and loud voice. when leaving
it traveled upward.
I am convinced this, unidentified Flying
Messenger or U.F.M. Has been
documented ,with noted encounters. in
our modern day, several times

Does this, in any way ,take any of Gods Glory away?

"No" it does not." God was as familiar with modern Technology then ,as we are now.!

We can all agree Jesus had Super Human abilities. very alien to this world.

What some cannot agree on, is where Reality verses the mystical .

I believe what ever mans mind, can imagine, mans mind can do.

with Gods agreement.

What is not Faith is Sin. Abraham was justified by faith.

Jesus walked on water .

Remember the time that passed ,from the time the boat set sail, after the two fish and five loafs of bread were eaten.

to the time Jesus arrived at the boat. I think he traveled at Super Sonic Speed.

And while he was moving, he was not "Walking."

I guess after covering the fact, that we are at least, part alien, and with faith we are

capable of things we can not imagine.
That we truly are Celestial, or Heavenly .
A Earthly kind of extraterrestrial

.

SEARCHING

Sheltered From all horizons,
Locked in my world of pride.
Lost   within myself, when I
Venture to the outer side.
Put on my mask of happiness,
Hide my tears in stride.
Sing Loud and laugh   No one knows the
tears I hide.
In shear   desperation. I grasp
For more   and more and find
What I been searching for,
Was always behind my own front door.

L.J.P

" HERE AFTER"
HEAVEN OR HELL

Still there is the" Here After" to consider
Heaven , Hell.,
    and the three words   HELL   was
translated from.

Old Testament.
       "SHEOL" translated constantly in
the Old Testament as HELL
(World of the Dead)
New Testament.
The New Testament   translated three
words into HELL.
    (1) TARTAROO (1st Peter 2:4) was the
only time used
        (Eternal Incarceration- or deep
Abyss)

(2) HADES In Revelations four times translated into HELL.

(unseen place of departed Souls)

(3)   "GEENNA" translated twelve times to HELL.

(Place of ever lasting Punishment)

" Heavenly" Celestial

(1) HEAVEN " Ouranos " Elevated Spirit, Power, Happiness Visible Orra

(2) Heaven   "Mesouranema "   MID SKY   only in Rev 8:13

(3)   Heaven   " OROS " Above any natural Rising

(4) REV: 8:13   Heavenly " Celestial " Beyond the Sky.
        Another Galaxy

Byseeing " STRONG'S CONCORDANCE" you can tell where each word is used.

PARADISE ETERNAL

There is so much, to be said,   for the good of this world. The beauty of mountains .

Streams , forrest   a   Creation of pure beauty. Man has enjoyed it for thousands of years.

When you think of all that we have deleted from this earth water, soil, vegetation.

We must know. We have used it up. God knew this oddly enough , the needs of our flesh

has   depleted , most of the things Man would need to

survive and it is happening at a high rate of speed. It seems to me, if we are to continue here , we would need to be absent the flesh. A Spirit Body could enjoy, what remains of the Earth

ENJOY THE PARK (EDEN)

I have always thought of ,my Spirit, in my, Celestial body, going over water falls,
walking through the Jungle. looking in caves , beneath   Earth. exploring the Sea floor
and a trip now and again to other planets.
No fiscal need for water , food, heat. Transportation,
I have heard said,   Heaven might be boring.
The only thing boring, is boring people. If   Heavenly or Celestial is far
Better than this Earth. I hope only happy people are there.
If a thousand years are as one day with God.

I have spent well over 25.500 days on Earth and not been board one

time. God has gave me motivation to spare. I try spreading it around.

I have spent my life being thankful for every breath. and Praise God for it.

So here is another" Apocalypse."

If there are any, who do not want to go where I go. It is their choice.!!!

DEVILS ADVOCATE

Religion has made a mockery of God's word. Using it to instill hate.
   intimidation . Using it to bully and even kill. This is a waste of time.
   There are always going to be those who make dogma, expecting others to live by it.
   I am so glad God gave us free will. When I hear of various Religious Wars I know the
   Adversary to God must be smiling.

   Like C .S .Lewis's " General Screw tape " and his letters
   Then I think of the ones who call them selves Christians

Catholic and Protestants killing one another back when I was young.

Then there are Muslims, Their God is Allah. APOCALYPSE.

The Daniel we read of in the Old Testament Called God Allah

(Which meant God in his language) Jesus spoke of another " Fold"

Before I Judge any . I want to be sure I have a right.

All the Religions I have studied seem to have , a Lord Jesus. Muhammad, Buddha, The Great White Father. That was most likely brown.

Jesus was most likely brown as, There are still , few white Nazarenes.

"Apocalypse" The only Soul we can correct is our own.

" Unless there is a question concerning God ", There is no need for a answer.!

God brought this understanding to me . He is fully capable of bringing it to others.

LOOKING FOR TRUTH
WHERE IO FIND IT

The Apocalypse I hope I have established as a Revelations ,or Light bulbs Moments, they

are nonstop for the , Thinkers, and Searchers. Some of what I understood

about the bible as a young person was due to false teachings. I was always a stickler for asking

where is the proof , the facts. If we are taught a certain way it is hard to go around it.

at a service once A Pastor speaking of the millennium, said from out of no where, "

There will even be babies born then. "!

I had always thought, this time would be a spiritual time. Flesh no more.

I questioned the pastor later asking, where he got that?   He said I will get the Chapter

and verse for you.! Weeks went by . Finally he came to me one day and explained how

busy he had been, but he had not forgot.

I said don't worry about it . " Its not there"

It would seem he heard this some where and believed it.

WINGS ON ANGELS

I said the Bible does not say Angels (Messengers) have wings" A elderly Pastor .

Said " Sister the Angel I saw had Wings"! I replied "I did not say your angel did not have wings." " I said the Bible does not say they do." A couple of others disagreed. with me. They were going to find it for me.

That Sunday after noon .

" They never did." ! Yet really Michael Angelo did paint them pretty. but a few Angels in my life would not have wanted to carry them around with them.

All the   mystical understandings have clouded the truth , in such a
way , that even the Elect   would be deceived. . If it were possible.

How can those who have no interest in learning the truth ever hope
to   Metamorphous into a Celestial body,

IS THERE A GOD GENE?

Could it be possible one day DNA will tell us
who is Celestial and who is not?

Could Abraham' s seed be detected?
So much to learn . Knowledge and
Technical

Understanding is advancing at warp
speed.

In 1960 a dear sweet aunt a Church
going lovable lady.

jumped on my case
one day, When I said " Soon we will
put a man on the Moon"

She quickly replied

"If God wanted men on the Moon he
would have put them there"

I replied . " He is " In 1969 I watched in

awe of the first step of a man on th e Moon.

Being afraid of change has become a religious Stigma.

Several times Jesus said "Fear Not" yet the unknown or unseen is often rejected

by Jesus believing Christians, lacking Gods Anointing. Or an Anointed Teacher.

Those called of God , are anointed to be called of God for Gods purpose. Too many selfdeclared teachers without Gods anointing .

Are blindly leading the blind.

The spiritual aspect is often ignored, and replaced with dogma , because this is all the

Teacher knows, and reaching beyond that understanding, is their worst fear

COULD DNA SEPERATE ANOINTED FROM UNANOINTED.?

Being afraid of change has become a religious Stigma.

THIS CHILD HAS NO SIN

One might think by all appearance that I
am alone,
One might even see me walking and
talking to no one.
Or think I am quite strange in my
personality. And Do no't know there is
another lives in side of me.
Directs me as I walk, guides my eyes and
ears, and in an instant if need be, desolves
my doubt and fears.
He puts me in rememberance of what I
should not do, and reminds me with a
check my mind has been renewed.
For with in me is a holy one, a spirit we all
share and if we do not grieve him, and in
Jesus Christ we pray.
He will utter to the father, this child has
no sin to day.

L.J.P.

IF GODS NOT TALKING
YOU'RE NOT LISTENING

Most do not hear God because they are afraid to say " God told me "

A long time I had the same problem. I had to start listening to my Spirit,

and this is on going .

I describe our Spiritual " APOCALYPSE " like this .

There was a terrible accident on the street, The way I usually go to town. Something told me to go another way.

I did and coming back ,

I came the usual way a horrible crash had happened,

it could have been me, had it not been for, Something telling me.

Instantly my Spirit confirmed who
something is.

Had I been taught of the Talking Spirit
I would have said" God told me"

MANY CALL GOD "SOMETHING"

There are other ways to look at this. God talks to you personally, seldom talks to someone   else through you.

In   my life time I have said things I know God told me,

because it was to profound, for my simple mind. Then someone else hears it and   acknowledge   the   profoundness of it.

Other times, I see how sometimes messages can get crossed up.

Once a Lady came to my door to tell me, that God told her Women should

not wear pants. I said   "   If God tells me that I will not do it "

"However he hasn't yet".!

Later I saw ,she had her long pants on. There are far to many of these.

That the Adversary will use . Ruin the Credentials of a Teacher

I have saw Televisions, Records, certain clothing piled and burned, because someone quoted God as saying   that these things need destroyed.

I study on the fact   that Tyndale wrote a book, that he said even a plow boy could read.

It was a translation of the New Testament. He was killed for it and the Books burned.

There was so much fear of him .

Christians dug him up burned his body and scattered his ashes .

No not Christians. No faith , Religious persons. With   fear of the unknown.

The world has came to be a world of Political Parties. and   as it should be every one has a opinion.

That is fine , until we try forcing our opinions on others. The U.S.A. over the

past has became divided concerning . certain elements , As being unacceptable to God.

And could be considered a Theocracy in the making.

Arguments from both sides have equal value.

Although the conservative approach is that if its bad ,

I do not intend to contribute to it.

Abortion is one such topic , Concerning Taxes.

Our personal feeling in no way should effect another's personal feeling.

God has gave us choices. Sometimes mankind. would like to

over rule God. Not understanding we each have a personal relationship with God.

and no one but God is to Judge

Joseph and Mary traveled to Bethlehem to pay taxes, as well as so many others.

They were not in a manger because they had no money.

Because there was no rooms left in town.

God told them they had to flea to Egypt for safety. Herod was killing all the baby boys

already born.   In this case would .
Abortion   would have been easier than
seeing your
    child slaughtered.

        " Would be a hard decision . One I
would want no part of."

DEATH NOT GODS WORK.

Blaming God for the loss of a loved one is all to often the norm .

And loosing a loved one, is hard.

For me it was important to know. Gods Children do not see death.

and as much as we long for them . We know they are with God in a

much more desirable state. So it makes mourning the loss, much lighter.

God did not create death, and in   fact over came it with his Son.

Knowing the return of the Holy Spirit would return them

to God from where they came .And death would no longer have power over them.

I have had two children in their prime
, who return to God . who trusted me with
them for a while, and while I miss them
so.

I can only Praise God knowing Gods
plan for us, is far greater than

any we have known on Earth.

For me it means my tribulation in my
flesh is only temporary. And my children
who are with God have tribulation no
more.

John was in tribulation when he was on
Earth.

WHAT IS NORMAL?

Normal depends on a certain place and time.

Paranormal,   is where ever normal for the time ,   is not.!

Seeing so many things in my life, become normal that would

have once been considered Paranormal, as a youngster, tells me every

new knowledge   or invention that progresses mankind,

Brings us one step closer ,to understanding our Celestial existence ,

as reality knowing God is our Celestial - Heavenly Father

And will eventually lead to another book by someone.

The same as when Jesus was   moving
Walking   on the waters

(Luke 6:49) and they supposed he   was
a Spirit.   Apparently it was not unusual to
see   apparitions

Ghost or Spirit at that time . " However
now it would be   Paranormal ."

" It was then."!

That same day Jesus fed five thousand
people, with five loafs of bread and two
fish.

That was very not normal, or Paranormal
Activity in one day

(Mathew 14) those five thousand followed
Jesus to the desert. After   hearing

Of John the Baptist being .beheaded   to
say the least in was a

abnormal   day   for all concerned

.

ARE WE   PREDESTINED
PRE ORDAINED?

Not against our own will.   This is not Gods
way,   freewill.

You   can ask God to Ordain you. And
predestine your life.

This is not credentials for Gods work.

Credentials are to appease man.

Long after I had been told a Woman
could not hold a office in church.

And by that time I had no desire to.

It occurred to me for the sake of my
daughters and   granddaughters

. this needed to be understood. I ask God
to guide me. And I was in a Ordination
Ceremony. Ordained to Gods word and
for his work, those who heard

Assumed I was going to Preach .

Even my own mother , though I corrected her often,

She would tell people I was a preacher.

Preacher translated correctly is Teacher.

And though I have officiated Marriage Ceremonies and Funerals.

I have never preached or evangelized it has as yet never been my calling.

at that Ceremony all my children were witness 's also my husband,

friends and cousins, to a manmade Ordination.

With a Ordained woman of God officiating.

I seldom reveal this, any more than I need to . Or other ceremonies

I have took part in.

I need no credentials to be a " Child of God " . Adopted through

The adoption of Jesus.

All who accept the blood of Jesus as their redeemer automatically belongs to God.

A Royal Priesthood a Holy Nation. No man can give this kind of Credentials.

And no Child of God will desire it from mankind.

The sad thing is without worldly Credentials , Religions will be unwilling to

accept anything from God, through you. No worry,

They would not listen to Jesus either. " Apocalyps e"

PET PEAVE

Something that has caused the hair on the back of my neck rise up.

To use the name of JESUS HOLY or GOD unnecessarily.

While playing a Game. or even watching one. I hear

"OH MY GOD" " JESUS CHRIST " HOLY you know what.
And neither of these have any thing to do with cause or effect.
It was always a teaching of mine , To use these phrases,
when talking to or about them.

A friend of mine use to do that I would say He had nothing to do with it.

As I told my Grandaughter. if you say "Oh my God"

repeatedly   without a reason.

One day you may need his attention,

and   he will assume you are not serious.

Like a little girl I saw patting her momies leg repeated saying mommy

Trying to get her attention. Mommy just set there staring into space.

I expected   this happens a lot with her.   Just a thought . I thought worth mentioning.

IN PARADICE today

The Apocalypse, and the death of Jesus have been
the most discussed topic among un committed ,
would be believers, It has not been well taught,
that every one, at some time has an apocalypse , or light bulb moment.
And that it should be shared.
The   Revelation received freely, should be taught freely.

As for the death of Jesus he was a sacrifice and as he told
the thief on the cross..
" TODAY YOU WILL BE IN PARADICE WITH ME "

Keep in mind he had not, been baptized or accepted Jesus as   Lord.

He was not a Member of any Church. or Religion.

However   he   believed   Jesus was truthful. and   the Son of God.

Jesus   Body , was the Temple of God.

Being destroyed . And remade in three days.

Paranormal

God not a respecter of persons

Since I do not consider my self religious . I
still see good in people who
    are steadfastly adhering to a dogma of
some sort, that at least acknowledges there
is
    a supreme God, It is my hope, they come
to know God personally

    As humans we are so narrow minded ,
to think ,
    we know the only right way. A friend
of mine in Egypt.
    I know has a loving Spirit that could
only come from God .
    In his language "Allah."
    The Book he believes in is different
than mine ,

Comparable to the old testament writings.

do not accept, Jesus as Son of God.

As does the Jewish Faith. I am not qualified to remark on either.

Since I have not studied it enough. It is not my calling to reform any ones belief.

I do consider myself able to discern spirits.

And in these faiths. I know there are some Holy.

God knows who has his Holy spirit , because there he is , sealed.

My faith is centered on that fact " That Emanuel " Is God with us.

" And I am one of us."

And that I offer ,the best example of a Christian that I can be.

Not with works always, but with Love, and the Truths God gives me.

I know I am God's . And all that is God's is Holy.

TONGUES or LANGUAGE

Taking part in the paranormal . Is the only way to define it.

you can be sure. if it is not normal , not many will agree with you.

as I said before a personal experience is just that personal.

The Word Tongues , in King James translation ,

Would have been better translated into language,

Has been considered to be evidence of the Holy Spirit.

I challenge that assumption, even though I do Pray in the Spirit.

Another language is of no value , if no one understands it.

I do believe you will see a difference, in ones conversation,

as the Holy Spirit begins to work with them.

Keep in mind on the day of Pentecost

as they all spoke on the streets. Observers from many ethnic and language,

understood in their own language. I conclude as they spoke they

anointed the ears of the hearers,

One step more . I say Messengers

who are anointed with the Holy Spirit

will anoint ears as they hear the words of messenger speaks.

Yes Paranormal. ! This is the Charisma Jesus had.

some say. I do not believe this, because many charismatic people

are for sure not Holy in any way.

This Celestial or Heavenly personality only the Children of God have.

Being of good report. Never fearing , loving even the unlovable.

and taking joy in helping others. Always with Godly intentions.

Old Testaments Paranormal Miracles.

This is my Testimony of what I have
observed and understood,

Of the New Testament Bible . Bringing
Old Testament story's

into this picture will explain , Paranormal
events, like the Burning Bush.

Abraham is told the Ground he stood on
was Holy.

Every where Abraham walked was
Holy.

He anointed the ground he walked on.

As can we. Claim dominion for God on
every thing we own

"And watch it be Blessed "

Consider the forty years of wandering.
same cloths ,

appearing   the same age   they relied
totally on God ,

took nothing with them. God supplied
their every need.

Their   faith   was tested. Now it's so
easy to see.

Hind   sight is pretty good, yet even
with all the knowledge

of their history we fall short of the
faith, God desires of us.

God   continuing   to love and bless us
, as only a Parent could.
   Because of the Blood of Jesus
The perfect sacrifice when Jesus paid
the   price
Until   next   time
God Bless the reader   by
Linda Pippin

IN MEMORY MY CHILDREN
God let me borrow.

AS YOU STEPPED IN THE TINY
TWINKLE OF AN EYE,
FROM NO MORE THAN A DREAM OF
THIS FRAGILE LIFE.
BACK TO REALITY, THE CELESTIAL
REALM ETERNAL'
YOU SEE MARY WEEPING AT JESUS
FEET.
AND GOD DECLARING EVILS
DEFEAT.
YOU WILL HEAR GOD IN A TINY
WHISPER,
YOUR SEED BLOOMED FROM THE
EPISTLES,
THROUGH GOD'S WORD, THE LIVING
LIGHT
YOU BECAME A MARVELOUS SIGHT.